悟の九段
A Journey Through
Nine Dans of Awakening

ButterflyMan

First paperback edition 2026

ISBN: 979-8-90217-023-5

Published by ButterflyMan Publishing LLC
United States of America

Website: https://www.butterflyman.com
Email: contact@butterflyman.com

Directory

Prologue: The Misty Mountain Path — Encountering "Dan"

- On a night mountain path, Sora stumbles into a wooden hut and meets an old man.
- The old man introduces the concept of "Dan": life as a journey of cultivation, rising from low to high.
- The seed of the "Nine Dans of Awakening" is planted.

Chapter 1: Shodan — Seeing the Tree, Missing the Forest

- At the office, Sora is trapped in details: he sees only "numbers," not direction.
- The old man uses the metaphor of "tree and forest" to guide him.
- Sora begins to reflect: why doesn't effort always lead to results?

Chapter 2: Nidan — Seeing the Mountain, Missing the Tree

- Sora begins chasing the "big picture," pursuing lofty visions.
- He reads motivational books, Silicon Valley legends, dreams of surpassing limits.
- But he falls into restlessness: "seeing only the mountain's shadow, neglecting the tree's roots."

Chapter 3: Sandan — Seeing Both Mountain and Tree

- He learns to connect the partial with the whole: caring for details without losing direction.
- For the first time, he persuades a client using the logic of "tree–branch–forest."
- Colleagues begin to notice his change.

Chapter 4: Fast Step — Wind, Action, and Rooting Deep

- A rival company suddenly takes the lead, throwing his team into crisis.
- With Haru introducing a consultant friend, Sora realizes: "others can see the mountain too; the key is speed and action."
- He learns to adjust in the wind, rather than being trapped in self-blame.

Chapter 5: Yondan — Seeing Mountain, Tree, and the Seasons

- Sora starts to see the dimension of time: mountain and tree are not only spatial, but seasonal.
- In project cycles he experiences ups and downs, seeing how wind, rain, and light shape the whole.
- The old man guides: wisdom flows with the seasons, not clinging to one moment.

Chapter 6: Godan — Seeing the Roots, Seeing Beyond the Mountain

- A global e-commerce giant alters its algorithm, shaking the industry.
- Sora discovers that "the winds outside the mountain" are the real tests.
- He learns to look downward at roots (supply chains, soil) and outward at winds (environment, uncontrollable forces).
- The old man concludes: "The wind cannot be controlled, but roots decide whether you endure."

Chapter 7: Rokudan — Action and Harmony

- Theme: wisdom made real.
- Sora tries to ground his insights into team, relationships, and life.
- A conflict and reconciliation with Haru teaches him: "Dan is not a solitary climb, but a shared walk."
- He begins to shoulder leadership responsibility.

Chapter 8: Nanadan — Return and New Departure

- Theme: transmission.
- Sora sees younger colleagues repeating his past confusions.
- He hesitates, then chooses to be a "light-holder."
- The old man gradually fades, hinting that the lineage has passed on.

Chapter 9: Hachidan — Emptiness

- Theme: non-attachment.
- On a solitary journey, Sora no longer rushes to find "answers," but accepts uncertainty and change.
- "Tree, mountain, roots, wind, seasons" merge within him, returning to emptiness.

Epilogue: Kyudan — No Dan

- Theme: infinity.
- At the end of Dans, there is "no Dan."
- Life has no final stage; everyone walks their own path of Dans.
- Sora matures into the figure of the "old man," but the lens does not linger—space is left for the reader.

Chapter One · Shodan: Seeing the Tree, Missing the Forest

Monday's sky looked faint, as if someone had rubbed it over and over with an eraser, thinning the blue into a damp white. Sora arrived twenty minutes earlier than usual. The office tower's sensor doors purred softly; inside, a custodial cart pushed a round-headed mop across the floor, drawing a narrow ribbon of wet light. He badged in. The elevator held only him, and in the mirrored walls four versions of himself appeared, all a bit too sleepy to be patient. As the car rose, it gave off a fine tremor—like a throat clearing.

The office was still cool; the AC had just woken and sent its first breath. Motion lights clicked on one by one, painting a belated band of white along the cubicle tops. Sora set his bag by the desk, fit his mug back into the faint circle on the coaster, booted up. The screen sprang a row of red dots to life: to-dos, nudges, approvals, meeting alerts... Little stubborn insects, clustering and twitching in the corner. He didn't open them yet. He warmed his palm and pressed it to the trackpad, as if soothing a small animal with a chancy temper.

In the half hour before stand-up, footsteps drifted in. The printer began first, grabbing and spitting paper, its puffing like the opening sprinkles of rain. At the long table, the coffee machine worked new beans; the grinding had a low grit to it, and the air lifted a fragrance that was neither sweet nor bitter.

"Morning." Haru came in with a backpack, hair a little mussed by the wind, jacket slung over his shoulder. "Beans don't taste as sour today."

Sora pointed beside him. "New lids on the second shelf to the left—don't scald yourself again."

"Oh." Haru bent to sniff the cup, then leaned back and lowered his voice. "Nine-thirty, Riku wants East vs. Central. Remember how he said 'no detours' last week?"

"Remember." Sora nodded. "I dropped last month's line so he won't say he can't see the focus."

"And," Haru slid his phone onto Sora's desk, "right after that you've got the product team's roadmap review. Might be tight."

Sora dragged a small gap into his calendar, five minutes between the two meetings. He reread the "quarter-straightened trend" page he'd built over the weekend, nudged the caption down a line to give the chart a bit more air. The cursor rested; for a moment he pictured that paper lantern at the steps rocking in night wind—something in him brushed lightly, then the new-mail ping flattened it.

By 9:15 most had arrived. Mika from Finance squared a stack of receipts and slid them into the reimbursement box; next door someone swapped a monitor, and when the plastic tie was snipped—"kak"—it landed like a period mid-sentence. Sora reviewed his deck order once more: agenda → overall curve → internal composition → channel comparison → competitor cadence → closing recs. Tiny page numbers in the lower right—black, thin, as if they didn't want to be noticed.

At 9:30 the glass door slid open. Riku twirled a marker between his fingers, wearing the look of someone who had memorized the map. A sweep of the room: "Okay, let's begin."

The first team was quick: KPIs in ten minutes. The second brought surveys, explaining a few choice distributions. Riku nodded now and then, sometimes writing two words on the board. When Sora's turn came, the lights seemed a notch brighter. He stood, plugged in the USB, and the cover page appeared.

"East and Central are overall stable quarter-on-quarter, but their internal structures are diverging," he began. "To avoid monthly noise, I've straightened the trend by quarter."
Next slide: clean lines, clear undulations. Sora's laser circled a bend. "This change starts mid-last quarter. On the surface it looks like organic growth, but split by channel and you see a structural shift."

Pens scratched. Eyes lifted. Riku said nothing; the marker rolled once in his palm.

Slide three: the channel comparison as bars—simple colors, differences obvious. Sora leveled his breath. "Recent Central growth stems from an increased weight in Channel B; East's lift comes mainly from Channel A's carryover effect."

"Hold on," Riku said. "You said 'mainly.' Based on what? Why not the other two lines?"

Sora paused, hovered the cursor at the legend—almost revealed the hidden "assist lines," then stopped his hand. He tried to pull the answer up whole. "It's the overlay of channel weight shifts and promo cycles. I removed the sharp spikes from short promos and kept the underlying trend."

"Fine. Sounds like you have a logic," Riku tapped the table, "but others can't see it. Put your 'removals' on a page. Don't make me guess."

"...Understood." Sora nodded, throat tight. The data wasn't wrong, but "others can't see it" wound through his windpipe like thread—no pain, just bind.

He pressed on—competitors' rhythm tweaks, price-band drift. Riku didn't interrupt again; on the whiteboard he wrote four dry strokes: LACKS DIRECTION.

The chalk letters stood upright, gridding the air. Sora stared a beat, then looked away. He threw up the final recs: "Short term, keep a conservative mix; avoid early reweighting in East. Mid term, watch Central's user-mix shift for its impact on repeat cadence."

"Mhm." Riku nodded, then shook his head. "You overworked this page. You built me a wall. I only need three things." He paused. "Also—open with why we're looking. Not everyone will grow a direction from your details."

"Got it," Sora said softly.

The meeting ebbed like a tide: chairs slid home, paper stacked, lids clicked shut. Sora pocketed the USB. A brush of his cuff on the table sparked static—like a pinprick from nowhere. Haru rounded past, brows pinched but smiling: "Not bad. Riku's in his 'direction doctrine' phase."

Sora smiled back, said nothing. He closed and reopened the laptop, revisited the "closing" page, bumped the line spacing by one, deleted two sentences. He realized he'd been trying to fill every white patch, terrified someone would say "not enough." Yet the board still had those four characters: lacks direction.

The glass door reflected corridor light, pasting a thin sheen over whoever walked out. Sora paused half a second at the threshold, as if a hidden board were strapped to his back. Someone slipped by, leaving a faint wash of hand soap, gone at once.

At his desk he opened the minutes and typed: "Add — show removal logic / front-load the 'why' / reduce closing density." At the word "density," he drifted: density was his talent—like weaving, he could lay warp and weft tight and true. But maybe some cloths should keep a seam for wind.

At 10:30 an email chimed: "HR Internal Training Signup." Three minutes later the product team shared "Next Month Roadmap Draft"—attachments of flows and swimlanes. He reached for his mug; the base thudded the coaster and he realized he hadn't drunk water all morning. The first mouthful was cool. He set the cup down and ran a finger around the rim, as if to confirm the boundary still held.

The printer jammed. Someone cracked the bay; the paper edge had a pale gray bruise from the rubber roller, a shadow pulled long. Mika hurried over and freed it in three quick moves, patting it flat. "Don't send such thick jobs," she said— quiet, measured certainty.

Watching that smoothed page, Sora felt an odd envy: some people knew how to ease what's "stuck" back on track—no rush, no rage, just untangle. He thought of the four chalk words, then of his page numbers pressed into corners, quiet as possible. Maybe, he thought, "quiet" and "direction" weren't opposites. He just hadn't found their handshake.

Ten minutes before noon, a ping from Riku: "4pm at my desk." "Roger," Sora replied.
The cursor blinked twice; calm returned. He re-laid the morning's charts, tossed a rough "removal logic" page into drafts, set a fifteen-minute reminder. The weather widget in the corner read "Cloudy → Sunny," a coin-small sun pinning the edge of a cloud.

By lunch the floor smelled different. Plastic lids peeled from bento; steam rose from rice, simple and warm. Haru set two onigiri on a napkin and handed one over. "Seaweed's crisp today."

"Thanks." Sora bit in—grains parted under his teeth; the nori carried the salt. Hunger, tardy but definite, arrived—a reassurance that the body was still here.

"That slide getting picked on was normal," Haru said, licking a stray grain off his finger. "He wants 'kick in the door.' You offered 'fully furnished room.' Next time, don't cram it—leave a gap he can walk through."

12

"Mm." No argument. He'd thought of leaving white space, but each time he cut out a hard-won block, a queasy insecurity rose from his stomach. Would others still "get it" once he removed it? The feeling was like not quite trusting he could find the path in a forest.

The afternoon tide of mail came silently back in. Sora tucked his head down—updated meeting links, confirmed a vendor detail, sent Finance two receipt images. His hand moved between keyboard and trackpad as if rubbing a map he couldn't see. Lines crisscrossed—close, far, parallel; he tried to trace them, but somewhere always stayed blank.

At 3:50 he closed most windows, opened the deck, roughed the "removal logic" page with "Supplement" at the top right, cut two explanations, left "for reference only." He didn't want it to look like a wall again. The reminder popped; he rose and headed to Riku's desk.

A big window at the corridor's end gathered an entire sky into glass. Wind shoved the cloud lightly; gray and white pressed together, and far off a ridgeline of blue peeked through. Sora passed a long table where someone had left a yellow sticky: rounded letters—"Projector, 9am tomorrow." He stared a moment, and a small, unimportant ease loosened his chest.

Riku's workstation was so tidy you wouldn't dare sit askew. The monitor's angle made a neat ratio with the desk edge— measured, surely. Riku nodded at the side chair. "Sit."

"Run the third slide again," he said without preface.

Sora brought it up. "This is the trend after removing short-term effects. To avoid—"

"Wait." Riku raised a hand. "Open with why—one sentence."

Sora stalled; a pebble lodged in his throat. He assembled it: "Quarter-straightening exposes the structural change and keeps us from chasing surface noise."

"Good." Riku nodded. "Now the chart. Remember, you're not looking alone—you're taking people with you. Tell them where you're leading from the first word."

"Got it." Sora exhaled and went on. He revealed the comparison layer, explained the removal rules, pointed out the gaps between two time points. "These short spikes—I kept them from dominating visual attention."

Riku watched two beats, then tapped the desk. "Next time, put this earlier. Don't make me reach slide three to see what your brain already did." He capped the pen. "And stop wallpapering your closing. I want three things: why look, what we saw, what we do. Not ten half-things like a honeycomb."

"Understood." Quieter now.

When Sora stood, his shoulders ached. The walk back wasn't long, but felt like it had more turns than in the morning. He sat and opened the to-do list, placing a small dot

in each box—"reorder charts," "front-load why," "reduce closing density." Not done—just marked: still in progress.

In the screen's reflection he saw his hands over the keyboard. A pale scar crossed one knuckle—maybe from moving boxes—he couldn't remember. It was so faint it barely showed under the light. He stared at that sliver of white and pictured time smoothing it from within. He didn't want to move, as if something needed to settle. Time moved anyway, prying a narrow lane through the office noise and pushing him toward the day's back half.

2) Afternoon Blank

After the morning meeting Sora's shoulders stayed stiff. He brought the "removal logic" page center screen again, trying to straighten his chain of reasoning per Riku's ask. Five minutes staring at the lines and his eyes pricked.

The cursor blinked on white, a small mouth asking over and over: Why? Why? Why?
He couldn't answer.

Post-lunch, bento scents hung in the air; the coffee machine sounded busier, like it was in a hurry. Haru rolled his chair over, chewing an onigiri. "You did fine, really. Still too hard-packed, though. You love counting every leaf in the forest."

Sora smiled faintly, didn't argue—just looked at the napkin. Something emptied inside.

Time flowed like a slow river, nudging him along. At 3:50 he went to Riku, filled in the page as told. Not much feedback; a nod, and: "Next time, put the why first."

Back at his desk he ticked a few boxes. Little checks like little nails, pinning him to the spot. However many nails, the ground still felt hollow beneath his feet.

3) Clocking Out

By six, the floor grew quiet. Lights still burned, but the air had gone cool—as if it had lost body heat. Sora tidied his desk, overturned his mug to dry on a cloth, shouldered his bag.

In the descending elevator a few colleagues compared weekend plans—new izakaya, a child's piano lesson, a travel promo. Not loud, but certain. Like they lived on a parallel map. Sora said nothing, just listened.

On the train, riders were scattered. Some scrolled; some dozed, shoulders swaying with the carriage. Outside was black, punctured by a few lights. Sora's reflection overlapped with others on the glass—faces blurred into one.

At eight he arrived at the small suburban station. Cool air after rain; a vending machine hummed.

Ahead: the familiar fork.

The south exit glowed steady, the street leading to convenience store, ramen shop, his small apartment—the most familiar route imaginable.

The north exit's lamps were sparse. Darkness opened its curtain toward the mountain's foot.

He stopped.

A thought flashed: If I go home, microwave a bento, then tomorrow will be meetings, charts, and those four words— lacks direction.

He sighed, turned, and walked toward the north exit.

4) The Path

It was strangely quiet outside the north exit. Long shadows stretched between the lamps; his footsteps lengthened into solitude. The wind combed through leaves. The path sloped upward; pebbles snapped underfoot.

He walked, but nothing inside loosened. Office images rose and fell—Riku's frown, the chalk letters, Haru's teasing. Thin films layered over his chest and wouldn't peel.

Fog pooled, swallowing the trees. Night pressed lower; the world smudged. Just as panic began to swell, a smudge of yellow appeared far ahead.

His heart caught. He quickened, following the light.

5) The Hut

The hut stood quiet on the hillside. Under the eaves a paper lantern swayed, light beating like a slow heart. On the steps, the old man still sat—gray robe, white hair a little mussed, serenity intact.

Sora approached. "Good evening," he said softly.

"Good evening." The old man nodded, eyes clear.

Then he smiled: "There are people here, and there is light."

Tea arrived again; steam drew a white thread under the lantern glow. They sat side by side on the steps. The wind moved, carrying a faint wood scent.

Sora cupped the warm ceramic. "Why do I always feel... not enough?" he asked. "I work so hard, but something's always missing."

The old man didn't answer outright. He lifted a finger and pointed into the fog at the ghost of a pine. "Look."

Sora looked—only vague branches. He frowned. "A tree."

The old man nodded and said no more, lowering his gaze to the lantern's shadow on the wood.

Sora waited long for an explanation that didn't come. Strangely, the confusion didn't spook him. It felt gently placed on a blank sheet—for later.

6) Down the Mountain

Night deepened; fog thickened. Sora rose to leave. The old man only nodded: "The road is here, and the light is here."

The path down was quiet. Bag on shoulder, his steps braided with wind. The fog remained, but the earlier panic had eased. The stone in his chest stayed—heavier, maybe—but truer.

At the foot he turned back. The hut blurred into mist, the lantern glowed like a patient star, hanging in the night.

He had no answers. He walked home slowly, the image of that pine still floating before his eyes.

Chapter Two · Nidan: Seeing the Mountain, Missing the Trees

1. The Passage of Time

Spring passed, and summer returned. Tokyo's streets grew muggy and damp in the rainy season, train cars heavy with the smell of wet umbrellas.

Sora's days, however, hardly changed: in the office he drowned in numbers, at night he dragged himself back to his apartment, where the fridge held little more than a few beers and frozen meals.

Since that night he had walked out through the North Exit, he often thought of the hut on the hillside and its paper lantern. *"A tree is a tree, a forest is a forest."* That vague phrase stuck in his chest like a nail, unsettling him.

He wanted to change, but didn't know where to begin. Until one day, at a subway convenience store, he picked up a glossy self-help magazine. On the cover, bold letters proclaimed:

"The Future Belongs to Those with Vision."

2. The Shock of Inspirational Stories

That evening, riding the train, he flipped through the magazine. It told the story of a Japanese entrepreneur: starting from selling clothes on a tiny online shop, becoming a billionaire in his thirties, and finally announcing plans to ride a rocket into space.

"Why?" the reporter asked.

The entrepreneur replied: *"Because Earth is too small. Humanity must look to a greater sky."*

Sora stared at those words, a flame catching in his chest. He thought of the spreadsheets and KPIs that filled his days, and suddenly felt small.

The article went on, recounting the investment stories of SoftBank's Masayoshi Son:
"Don't look only at three years, look at thirty. Don't look only at products, look at humanity's future."
Even at his most difficult times, Son had poured billions into a struggling company, simply because he believed in its vision.

Wedged into a cramped train seat, Sora felt a giant force shoving him forward. He closed the magazine, repeating silently to himself:

"I must learn to see the big picture. I must learn to be like them."

3. A Shift at Work

Weeks later, Sora's colleagues began noticing his presentations had changed.

Before, he always arrived with thick stacks of data, decimal points polished to perfection, every fluctuation dissected to the last detail. Now, he often cut half the slides and began with declarations like:

"In the next five years, we must rethink our approach."
"The market is not a pile of numbers, but a flow of trends."
"We must move like Silicon Valley—let vision drive action."

The room fell into silence.
Someone coughed. Another traded glances.

Riku's brows knitted. He tapped the table. "Big words. But specifics? Where's the data? Where's the plan?"

Sora opened his mouth, only to realize he hadn't prepared details. His words collapsed into silence.

After the meeting, Haru tugged his sleeve, half-joking: "What's gotten into you lately? One day it's trees, the next it's mountains, now you're trying to be a Silicon Valley founder? Don't get carried away."

Down the hall, two colleagues whispered:

"Is he cracking under pressure? Losing it?"
"He used to obsess over decimals, now it's all big-picture speeches. Weird shift."

Sora heard them but pretended not to. His chest tightened, yet stubbornness rose: at least he was no longer the man who lost himself in tiny details.

4. Lonely Nights

Late at night, he sat alone at his desk in the apartment. On it lay his latest purchases: *Ten People Who Changed the World*, *The Secrets of Success*, *The Next Thirty Years*.

The pages declared:

"True leaders don't fixate on today—they see a hundred years ahead."
Another line: *"Your scope determines your height."*

Sora couldn't help imagining: if one day he stood on a stage, igniting thousands with a single sentence, what would it feel like?
He even practiced in the mirror: *"The future is not just numbers—it is direction."*

But in the next instant, he remembered the meeting room: Riku's cold questioning, Haru's teasing glance, his colleagues' murmurs.
At that moment, he felt like a clown.

He swung between dream and reality like a pendulum— forever searching for balance, never finding it.

5. Friday Night

One June Friday, Sora worked late again. By nine, the building had mostly gone dark, leaving only him and a few humming machines. He shut his screen, shoulders aching.

Outside, the streets glistened with leftover rain. In the damp air, a billboard blinked a slogan:

"Look to the Future: Vision Shapes Destiny."

Sora stared at it, a bitter smile tugging his lips.
For months he had practically memorized such slogans as mantras. Yet in reality, they felt hollow shells.

He descended into the subway, pushed toward the South Exit with the crowd.
The oden at the convenience store steamed; the ramen shop lantern swayed in the breeze. He had walked this route countless times.

But he stopped.
That familiar tightness clamped his chest.

Lifting his head, he saw the sign for the North Exit. The arrow pointed into darkness, like a summons.
After a few seconds, he turned, walking toward the North Exit.

6. The Mountain Path

Outside the North Exit was silence. The air cooled by rain; the stone path shone wet. Wind brushed the leaves into whispers.

He walked in the dark, two voices surging inside:

The books: *"The next thirty years..."*
Riku: *"Empty words are easy to say."*

Fog rose and swallowed the path. He felt caught in a net, tugged between dream and reality.

At last, a faint yellow glow appeared ahead.
The hillside hut. A paper lantern swayed, light pulsing like a slow heart.

7. The Hut

On the steps, the old man still sat. Gray robe, white hair stirred by wind.

Sora approached, lowered his voice: "Good evening."

"Good evening." The old man nodded.

"And here—there are people, and there is light."

They sat side by side. Steam rose from tea, parting the night.

Sora cupped the cup, and the words tumbled out: "I've tried to look at the big picture. I echo visions, futures. But they say it's empty talk. Am I wrong?"

The old man didn't answer right away. He lifted a hand, pointing toward the mountain shadow blurred in fog.

"What do you see?"

"A mountain."

The old man nodded, then pointed at a slick stone by his feet. "And this?"

"A stone."

Softly he said: "If you only look up at mountains, stones will trip you. If you only stare at stones, the mountain will slip away."

Sora froze. He didn't understand it all, yet something inside him was gently nudged.

8. A Metaphor

After a while, the old man handed him the cup.
"When flowers bloom, it is the soil that sustains them. When mountains rise, it is stones beneath that hold them."

Sora didn't grasp it fully. But the words sank like seeds, quietly buried in his chest.

9. Descent

Night deepened. Sora rose to leave.
The old man smiled: "The road is here. The light is here."

The path down was quiet. Fog scattered the lamps, his footsteps echoing alone.
He had no answers, only heavier questions.

But this time, he didn't panic.

He knew he was walking into another chapter of his training.

At the mountain's foot, he turned back. The hut blurred into mist; the paper lantern glowed like a patient star, quietly suspended in the night.

Chapter Three · Sandan: Seeing Both Mountain and Tree

1) Before the Meeting: Paper and Heartbeats

Thursday night. The floor was half dark, lights scattered.
Sora spread two decks across his desk:

- **Plan A**: rows upon rows of data, splits, comparisons—like flying low enough to touch every leaf: the "tree method."

- **Plan B**: three slides of "Vision → Direction → Execution"—like climbing high for the wide view: the "mountain method."

He flicked back and forth between the two, heartbeat rising and falling with the cursor.
In the screen's reflection, the crease between his brows seemed lighter than months ago, but it hadn't disappeared.

He thought of Zen's tea: on the surface of the cup, tree-shadows and mountain-shadows lived together.

So he made a **third deck**—stitching the two languages: start from a store display, zoom to a region's structure, then drop back down to the next concrete step.

Softly he read it aloud, like speaking to an empty apartment:

"When a single leaf turns, the whole tree's light and shadow change. We don't get lost among the leaves, nor do we talk only in the clouds. We walk along the branch."

Still, his chest stayed tight: if Riku turned on him, any "stitching" could be flattened by one line—**"Stop telling stories."**

2) In the Meeting: A Thump on the Table, and Silence

Friday morning.
The projector flared; the air pulled taut like a string.
Sora opened with store photos, then paired them with an 18% rise over three days.
"This is only one detail," he paused, "but it reminds us: when a single leaf turns, the whole tree's light and shadow change."

Riku didn't cut him off.
So he continued:

- **Slide 2**: mapped the store action onto subtle shifts in channel structure.
- **Slide 3**: placed that structure inside the quarter's rhythm.
- **Slide 4**: pulled it down into "three things for next week."

"We're not here to tell a pretty story," Sora lowered his voice before the close.
"We're here to make the story happen."

For a moment, silence. Only the hum of the AC.

"Not bad." Riku, for once, didn't call it "too shallow" or "too vague." He tapped the table with his pen.
"This afternoon—client meeting. You're taking the front."

The words landed. Heads lifted. To take the front was both recognition and trial by blade.
From the corner, Haru shot him a wink: **Hold steady.**

26

3) Break Room: Wind and Rumors

Afterward, cup lids clicked in the pantry.
"He's like a different person lately."
"Nice talk, but who knows if it sticks?"
"When people change, others won't like it. That's all."

Haru said nothing. He handed Sora a cup of warm water.
"Don't let the wind carry you. The wind shifts."

Sora nodded, though inside he rippled: wind—sometimes applause, sometimes gossip.

4) Pre-Client Surprise: A "Wrong" Table

1:30 p.m. A backend colleague rushed up, face white as paper. "This morning's East-region display table—the second column baseline—it's last month's spec. Needs today's update."

Sora's mind thudded.
That slide was his arrowhead. With the corrected spec, 18% shrank to **12%**.

Haru whispered: "We can pull it, salvage now. But the client pitch collapses. Push it through, and you might be exposed live."

Sora stood like on a broken bridge. He shut his eyes two seconds: **If leaves turn, the tree's light shifts.**

"Change it." He opened his eyes.
"Put the real number. Then explain why it fell: half from store action, half drained by platform activity. We tell cause, not dress the figure."

"But clients want the shiny story!" the backend panicked.

Sora shook his head. "They want a believable story."

5) Client Meeting: High and Low, Heavy and Light

The meeting room lights were harsher. Opposite, three clients smiled like porcelain masks.

Sora went up.

Slide 1: photos.
Slide 2: **12%**—not 18.

Brows rose.
He didn't flinch. He broke down the fall—platform campaign siphon, baseline update, display adjustment effects.

"If all we need is good-looking slides, we can stick to the old spec." He paused.
"But if we want results, we need to know where the light comes from, where the shadow falls."

The room stilled.
The woman in the middle snapped her pen closed, nodded once. "Go on."

In the second half, Sora laid out the structure: **leaf → branch → crown → forest.**
Then back to "three things for next week":

1. Recalculate ten benchmark stores with the new baseline.
2. Review platform rhythm versus display tweaks.
3. Bundle replicable display patterns and pilot in sample regions.

Riku stayed silent, only nodded at key points.

At the end, the woman said: "Thank you for using not the prettiest numbers, but the truest reasoning. We'll allocate a test slot next week."

At the door, Haru nudged him with an elbow. "You won."
Sora smiled, sweat cooling on his back. "Not a gamble," he thought, "just bringing the wind back to ground."

6) Back at the Office: Wind Turns Again

At his desk, the internal chat already lit with a screenshot: *client praise.*

- "Sora delivered."
- "Carried the day."
- "Even 12% spun into a story—impressive." (dripping irony)

Haru spun his chair. "Don't swallow it. Wind through trees always carries the sound of leaves."
Sora laughed. "I know. Leaves rustle—the trunk must stay firm."

Then Riku walked by. Only one line:
"Monday, review. You lead. Don't relax."

Not reward. A new stone laid in his path.

7) Night · Dream: Towers and Streets

Back home, Sora collapsed in his chair without turning on the light.
A mail popped: **test slot confirmed.**

He exhaled hard, throat parched.
After washing, he flipped a book. A line: *"In one leaf, see a whole season."*

He shut the cover, closed his eyes. Half-dream, half-wake:
He stood atop a skyscraper, city lights flowing like a river.
He looked down for streets—then saw someone below, looking up.
The gaze was his own: reverence for horizons, fear of the next curb.
Wind tore his coat. He tried to speak, but only water filled his throat—like tea trembling in a cup, tree-shadow in the base, mountain-shadow along the rim.

He jolted awake. A wet leaf clung to his window, then slid down with the rain.
He remembered Zen's finger resting on the curve of a cup: **a vessel can hold two worlds.**

8) Weekend · Small Things: One Grain, One Field

Weekend overtime brought cafeteria meals.
Behind the counter, a masked cook heaped rice and said, "Eat more, young man."
Sora thanked him—then thought: *in one grain of rice, a whole field.*

Through the steam: a rushed kitchen, relentless shifts, prices and weather down the chain.
A bowl of rice is never just a bowl of rice. It is many unseen hands.

Later at a convenience store, a schoolgirl fumbled coins; one 1-yen piece rolled under the counter.
Flustered, she bowed apologies, bent to search.
Sora crouched, handed it to her. "Here."
She smiled shyly. "Thank you."

Outside, wind rattled his plastic bag. He thought: the tiniest coin can tip an account. **If details fail, the whole cannot stand.**

This too was leaf, this too was trunk.

Countless small acts gave the air its order, its clean scent—and that order flowed back into clients' screens, into reports, into the credibility of "direction."

9) Monday · Review: Highs and Lows

The review meeting soured at once. A partner team snapped: "You breezed through the pitch, while backend carried the mess! Specs changed again and again—who takes the blame?"

The air turned coarse.
Sora didn't bite. He held out a marker: "Show us the potholes. The more concrete, the better."

The man hesitated, then drew: interfaces, specs, time windows, coverage—roots.
Sora added:

"Next week, we unify roots in one doc: who writes, who reviews, who releases. Front of the board. From roots, grow branches: product tables, regional spec differences. Weekly checks. If roots wobble, leaves fall. If roots hold, even wind becomes song."

The pressure eased.
Riku this time didn't say "not bad." Only one word: "Good."

Afterward, by the window, he said quietly:
"Next quarter, you lead the first half."

"Mm." Sora answered, stone pressed lightly on his chest. Not a gift. A test.

31

10) Autumn Night · North Exit: Wind Rises

Friday night, wind heavy.
Sora paused at the turnstile, then stepped north.

Streetlamps shivered. Ginkgo leaves spun down like golden whispers.

The mountain road was darker, stones wet, soles slipping.
Halfway, wind surged, snuffing out a lamp under the eaves.
He froze—the road ahead blackened deeper.
He thought of retreat—then heard a faint water-sound in the wind, like tea cooling by breath.
He kept on.

11) The Hut: Two Worlds in a Cup

The paper lantern swung shallow in the wind. The old man sat steady on the steps, like a stone holding the gust.

"Good evening." Sora's breath carried chill.
"Good evening." The elder gestured for him to sit.

A cup pressed warm to his palm—tea hot, rim cool.

"Wind is strong today."

Sora nodded. "It blew out a lamp along the path."

"But you still arrived," the old man said.

Silence. Wind brushed the eaves, lantern humming soft.

After a while, he blew across his tea. Ripples spread: the cup first held the roof's edge, then the nearby tree, then the faint mountain—layers resting in one vessel.

"Tell me—does this cup hold only the tree, or only the mountain?"

Sora stared: neither before nor after. Tree and mountain quivered together at each breath of wind. He swallowed, didn't answer.

The old man only turned the cup a fraction. "See? Angle changes, shadow shifts. Cup remains the same."

The wind rose and fell, like someone smoothing invisible paper.

"This week I saw two winds," Sora said suddenly. "Applause, and ridicule. Both loud."

The old man nodded. "Both can snuff a lamp."

"What then?"

"Put the lamp lower."

He pointed: at the steps below stood a smaller, steadier lamp. No wind could touch it.
Sora lowered his eyes, smiled faintly: put the lamp lower.
Not shrinking vision—rooting it closer to the soil. The soil held roots.

The old man handed him another cup.

"Tomorrow, in one grain, see the field. In one spec-sheet, see the forest. Write roots clearly—then leaves will dare to grow."

Light caught in Sora's eyes. "Roots..."

"Written so even strangers can understand," the old man added, tapping like a nail into wood.

12) Down the Mountain: Light and Weight

The wind eased. Sora rose.

"The road is here, the lamp is here," the old man said.

The path down felt clearer than before. Shadows crossed and traded places under swaying branches.

He walked unhurried, as if listening to a song with drumbeat: feet in light and heavy alternation, ears in highs and lows.

At the corner, the lamp blown out earlier glowed again—wind ceased, or system reset.
He didn't dwell, only nodded inwardly: the lamp was still the lamp.

At the foot, he turned. The hut blurred in mist, lantern heartbeat slow, steady.

In his chest, the stone lightened, a patch lifted, exposing warm soil beneath.

Tomorrow—write the roots of the spec-sheet clear.
Next week—grow the leaves of the display plan firm.
Next quarter—let the wind itself sing in tune.

He didn't think of farther mountains.
He lowered the lamp, and walked forward.

Chapter Four · Yondan: Swift Steps

Wind Rises · Action · Deep Roots

1. Wind Rises

Autumn in Tokyo always arrived without sound.
By the Kanda River, the ginkgo leaves turned yellow overnight, like someone had spilled a golden river on the ground. The wind carried a chill, scattering the smell of cigarette smoke outside the convenience store.

But in the office, the air was heavy, almost stifling.

That morning at ten, news suddenly came from the marketing department, and the entire floor erupted:

> "The competitor has already launched their promotion in the West District."
> "It looks almost identical to what we were preparing."

> Whispers flitted between desks.
> "Was our plan leaked?"
> "If only we had moved faster."

> In the meeting room, the atmosphere froze.
> Riku snapped his folder shut with a loud *thwack* and said coldly:

"Sora, you follow up."

The words landed like a nail.

Sora froze, fingertips icy. The West District promotion had been their next planned move, but the opponent had seized the first step. It was like a crucial piece on the board being taken away.

He understood: if he didn't handle this well, not only would they lose the client's trust, the entire project might collapse.

It felt like a stone pressed against his chest, making it hard to breathe.

2. A Shoulder in the Night

Tokyo after overtime was like a cauldron of boiling black. Neon lights shimmered across the rain-slick streets; crowds pushed down into the subway entrance.

Just as Sora was about to enter the station, a voice called from behind:

"Hey, wait."

It was Haru.
His expression was calm, but the concern showed between his brows.

"Don't bottle it up," he said. "I've got someone lined up—let's grab a drink."

They went to an old izakaya in Kanda. The wooden door slid open, releasing the smells of soy and oil. The yellow light was dim, the air warm with the comfort of food and smoke.

At the table sat a man in his thirties, suit jacket open, tie loosened.

"Haru's college classmate," Haru introduced. "He's at an independent consulting firm now. Thought it'd be good to chat."

After a few rounds of drinks, the man said casually:

"Your strategy itself isn't wrong. Looking at the past few months of data and industry trends, anyone could have worked it out. The competitor just moved faster—they have fewer constraints, so they can act immediately."

Sora listened quietly.
So his so-called "unique discovery" was not unique at all.
The difference was simply—**others were faster.**

When they left the izakaya, the night wind cut cool across their faces.
Haru patted his shoulder. "Don't be too discouraged. At least it shows your vision was right."

Sora said softly: "Haru, thank you. Not just today. These days, every time I've been close to breaking, you've shown up."

Haru smiled. "It goes both ways. I need someone to remind me too—not to stare only at the stars and forget the road under my feet."

On the train ride back, the two stood shoulder to shoulder. The carriage swayed, the light flashing across their profiles.
Silence was no longer distance—it was a quiet companionship.

3. A Trial of Action

Monday's weekly meeting.

This time Sora didn't pile the screen with data tables. Instead, he proposed a concrete pilot:

"Let's select ten stores, package the display plan into a reusable format, and review results within a week."

Someone frowned. "A week is too short. The numbers won't mean much."
Sora shook his head. "If we wait a month, the competitor will already copy it. Only by moving fast can we know if the roots hold."

Whispers rippled around the room.
Riku didn't dismiss it. He said coldly: "Then let the results speak."

For the first time, Sora felt a sense of resolve.
Swift steps weren't slogans. They were steps you actually took—proof written in results.

4. Trial in the Wind

One week later, the pilot data came out.
Sales had risen **12%**. Not the dazzling 18% he once imagined, but grounded and traceable.

At the client meeting, Sora put the real numbers on the screen.

"This is our three-day test. Half of the lift came from display, half was offset by platform activity."
The client raised a brow. "Only 12%?"

Sora didn't flinch.

"If all we wanted were pretty numbers, we could stick with the old baseline.
But if we want results, we must know where the light comes from, and where the shadows fall."

The room paused for several beats.
Then the client in the center snapped her pen shut and nodded. "Go on."

By the end, she said, "We'll allocate a test slot next week—use your plan."

At the door, Haru grinned and punched Sora lightly in the arm. "You carried it."
Sora's back was still damp with sweat, but his heart felt steady: this wasn't gambling—it was bringing the wind back down to the ground.

5. The Lesson of Deep Roots

That night, Sora walked the mountain path again. The wind was stronger, tossing the paper lantern back and forth.

At the hut, the old man sat on the steps, steady as a stone anchoring the storm.

"The wind is strong tonight," the old man said softly.

Sora nodded. "Yes. Wind can blow out a lantern."

"But it cannot move a tree with deep roots." The old man passed him a cup of tea.

On the tea's surface, the eaves, a tree's shadow, and a distant mountain overlapped within the same water.

"Change the angle, and the shadows change. But the cup remains the same," the old man said, gently turning it.

Sora stared at the shifting reflections. For the first time, there was no impatience in his chest.

He said quietly:

"Swift steps aren't just for speed. They're for sinking roots."

The old man smiled faintly and said nothing more.

Chapter Five · Yondan: Seeing the Mountain, the Tree, and the Seasons

Rhythm · Balance · Cycle

1. Early Winter in Tokyo

Winter in Tokyo always comes without warning.
Stepping out of the subway in the morning, the wind funnels between the towers, sharp enough to sting. In Shibuya, neon still blazes, young people line up for coffee in thick coats, but their steps are quicker than usual.

Sora carried his folder, his palm stiffened by the cold air.
For the first time, Riku had given him a direct order:
"Next quarter's first half—you lead."

He hadn't replied with more than a murmur.
But in his heart he knew: this wasn't a reward, it was an exam.

2. The Struggle Before the Meeting

Thursday night, the office was half-dark.
Most had gone home; only the hum of printers and air vents filled the corridor.

Sora laid two plans across his desk:

> • **Plan A**: spreadsheets over ten pages, every channel's margin mapped—like chopping the forest into countless branches and leaves.

• **Plan B**: three slides—Vision, Direction, Execution. A mountain's outline, clean and simple.

He toggled back and forth, heartbeat chasing the cursor near and far.
In the reflection of the screen, the crease between his brows looked shallower than months ago, but still there.

He remembered the old man's tea: the surface holding both tree and mountain.
So he tried a "third way"—a stitched plan: start with a small action in one store, scale to a region's structure, then land in three tasks for next week.

Alone in the empty meeting room, he read aloud quietly, as if speaking to himself in the dark:

"When one leaf turns, the whole tree's shadow shifts. We don't get lost among the leaves, nor float above the clouds. We walk along the branches."

Yet he knew: if Riku turned cold, even this weaving could be undone by one phrase—"don't tell stories."

3. Metaphor in the Meeting

Friday morning, the conference room glowed cold-white.
The projector lit, pulling the air taut like a string.

Instead of diving into numbers, Sora began with four images:

• Spring—sakura blooming over a shopfront draped with flags;
• Summer—under blazing sun, the cold drink case crowded with customers;
• Autumn—ginkgo leaves drifting, shelves dressed in warm colors;

42

• Winter—snow at night, shop windows glowing soft gold.

"Details are leaves of the season; strategy is the mountain," he said slowly.
"But if we only see one season, we forget the cycle. The true strength lies in seeing all four."

Then he layered: a week's pilot data → mapped into a quarter's rhythm → aligned to yearly goals.

As if putting "the shadow of a leaf" into "the turning of the seasons."

The room went still.
Riku did not interrupt. The client reps glanced at each other but didn't push back.

Sora's palms were damp, but steadier than before.

4. A Blow

Soon after, bad news arrived:
Another region's pilot had failed—sales didn't rise, but fell by 3%.

Whispers spread:

"Just a fluke?"
"Maybe the model's broken?"
"Should we bury this and not report it?"

The wind had shifted, scattering nerves.

Sora said nothing at first, staring at the downward chart.
After a few seconds, he spoke:

"Failure has to be part of the whole. Spring isn't only blossoms. Winter must count, too."

The room paused.
Riku gave no opinion, only a curt: "Next week's review—you present."

5. The Whisper of the Break Room

At lunch, the break room hummed with fragments.

"He's good at telling stories now."
"Stories sound nice—can he really deliver?"
"People change, some won't like it."

A snicker here, a shake of the head there.
Haru stayed quiet, handed Sora a cup of hot water, and said softly:
"Don't let the wind carry you. It always shifts."

Sora nodded, though ripples rose inside:
The wind could be applause, or gossip.

6. Walking the Night Path

On the weekend, Sora returned to the mountain path.
The wind cut colder; the trees were nearly bare. The paper lantern swung softly in the draft.

The old man sat on the steps, cradling a lamp—like a stone holding the night steady.

"The wind is colder," he said, gazing at the silhouettes at the horizon.

"Yes," Sora exhaled white breath, "the ginkgo is almost gone."

He thought of the company's falling chart, and added quietly:

"One region up, another down. Like the seasons—it can't all be spring and summer."

The old man didn't answer immediately. He blew across his tea; the surface quivered, reflecting first the eaves, then a withered branch.

At last, he spoke:

"The seasons aren't four answers, but one cycle. Trees need winter to grow; mountains need frost to stand. If you only love spring and summer, and can't endure autumn and winter— you haven't seen a real forest."

Sora watched the shadow in the tea. His chest felt gently pressed.
Failure wasn't an end. It was part of the cycle.

7. Realization

On the way down, the wind still moved.
Behind him, the lantern swayed—like a heart, steadying its beat in the gusts.

For the first time, Sora felt a widening calm:
Action mattered, but more than that—accepting the rhythm of the seasons.

- Spring to sow,
- Summer to grow,
- Autumn to harvest,
- Winter to sink and rest.

Projects, like lives, must turn with the cycle.

Metaphor

Those at **Fourth Dan · Seeing the Mountain, the Tree, and the Seasons** understand:

- The big picture must be watched, the details still guarded.
- More important is to know the rhythm of cycles.

Speed isn't everything. Stability isn't everything.
Only by flowing with the turning seasons can trees green year after year, and mountains stand evergreen.

Chapter Six · Godan: Seeing Roots, Seeing Beyond the Mountain

1. The Omen of Wind

In early winter Tokyo, the wind always arrived without warning.
Overnight, the gingko leaves along the streets turned golden. A single gust sent them raining down, carpeting the ground like a river of gold.

On his way to work, Sora slowed his steps. The wind whistled in his ears. It didn't feel like just another turn of the seasons—it felt like a message.

Inside the office, however, the atmosphere was entirely different.
At the morning meeting, the marketing team announced news that shook the floor:

"Clients want us to explain the abnormal sales these two weeks."
"Growth had been stable, and now it's plummeted."

Someone pulled up the charts. The red downward line cut through the screen like an open wound.

"Did our data baseline go wrong?"
"Or did a competitor pull something?"

Riku said nothing at first. His gaze swept across the room, cold and sharp, before landing on Sora.
"You check."

Sora's heart sank.

This wasn't just a "data glitch." It felt like the beginning of a storm.

2. Crisis: The Invisible Hand

Sora pulled six months of data into a massive sheet.
At first, everything looked normal—the growth curve followed their forecast, rising steadily. But two weeks ago, it nosedived, as if an invisible hand had swept it off the board.

He stared at the screen, and a news headline from the night before flashed in his mind:

A global e-commerce giant had just adjusted its recommendation algorithm.
On the surface, it was only a tweak to homepage displays, but overnight, merchants' sales rankings were reshuffled.

A chill ran down his spine.
This was **"the wind beyond the mountain."**
The problem wasn't internal. It was a butterfly flapping its wings across the ocean.

In the meeting, voices clashed:
"How do we tell clients? Just say 'someone changed their algorithm'?"
"This is uncontrollable. Who could have predicted it?"

Riku finally spoke, voice like steel:

"If the roots aren't deep, the wind can tear out the tree."

Silence fell.
Sora's chest tightened. Was it really just weak roots? Or had they failed to see beyond their own mountain?

3. Exploration: Beneath the Roots

That week, Sora barely slept.
Alone in the office, he stripped data layer by layer. Not only sales figures—but deeper flows: supply chain shipping cycles, logistics delays, currency fluctuations, even how weather affected storage.

He realized for the first time:

In the past, he only saw **leaves**—the daily numbers dancing.
Later, he learned to see **trees**—market trends.
Then, he learned to see **mountains**—the industry landscape.

But now, finally, he touched **roots**.

A tree's strength lay not in its branches, but in its roots.
Roots tied into soil's water and minerals, into climate cycles, even into tectonic shifts.

One algorithm tweak, one supply chain delay—these could jolt an entire forest.

He scribbled in his notebook:

"The wind cannot be controlled. But the roots decide if we withstand it."

4. Night Visit: Return to the Hut

Friday night, he climbed the mountain path again.
The wind was fierce, trees swaying, shadows lunging across the stone steps. Yet the hut's paper lantern still glowed, steady as a heartbeat.

The old man sat on the steps, gray robe rippling in the gusts.

"Good evening," Sora said, sitting down, breath cold from the climb.

The old man handed him tea. The rippling surface mirrored eaves, branches, and a faint mountain line.

"What did you see in the wind?" the old man asked.

Sora watched the reflection. Slowly, he said:
"The tree shakes, but the roots remain."

The old man nodded.
"The wind may come from beyond the mountain. But the roots live within it."

Wind swept under the eaves. The lantern swayed but did not go out.
In that moment, Sora understood: storms cannot be avoided. But survival depended not on their size, but on the depth of roots.

5. Turning Point: Seeing Beyond the Mountain

At work, arguments still raged.
Some insisted on clinging to old baselines: "Clients only want stable answers."
Others wanted to chase the new trend, scrambling to pivot.

Two gusts of wind colliding in a conference room.

Sora offered a third path:

"We must do both.
First—deepen our roots: unify data baselines, audit supply chains, secure stability.
Second—lift our eyes beyond the mountain: track global platform rules, watch shifts in consumer habits."

He paused, meeting their eyes.

"We cannot control the wind. But we can decide how deep our roots go."

For a moment, silence.
Then Riku nodded. "Try it."

For the first time, Sora felt his words weren't "analysis," but something others could trust.

6. Outcome: Wind Stops, Light Holds

A week later, they delivered the new model.
It couldn't predict every swing, but it explained causes: which were internal, which were **winds from beyond the mountain.**

The client listened quietly. At the end, she said:
"Data is not an oracle. But your explanation gives peace of mind."

That sentence carried more weight than any "perfect figure."

The office atmosphere shifted.
Some began trusting his judgment. Whispers spread: "He really does see farther."

Sora didn't feel proud.
He knew the wind would return.

7. Epilogue: The Heartbeat of Roots and Wind

On the weekend, Sora walked the mountain path again.

The wind was harsher, gingko leaves pelting like golden rain against the stone steps.

The hut still glowed.
The old man passed him tea. The cup reflected branches and mountains—but this time, Sora looked deeper, as if glimpsing the unseen root system beneath the soil.

"Beyond the sound of wind, leaves, and mountains," the old man murmured,
"there is also the heartbeat of roots."

Sora didn't reply. He only whispered inwardly:

"Every flap of wings in the world becomes wind. Only deep roots survive it. Only by seeing beyond the mountain do we escape the prison of our forest."

Wind blew. The lantern swayed lightly—yet still burned.
Sora raised his cup. For the first time, he felt it clearly: wind and roots, trees and mountains, inside and outside—no longer opposites, but one whole world.

Chapter Seven · Rokudan: Action and Union

1. Aftermath

December in Tokyo grew sharper, the wind cutting colder by the week.

The ginkgo trees had shed their last leaves, leaving bare branches along the streets. Walking home late from overtime, Sora often thought of the city as a winter tree—its exterior bleak, but roots beneath the soil quietly drawing strength.

He thought the stage of Godan would steady his heart.
Instead, the deeper he walked, the more he found the path demanded *union* with others.
That, strangely, unsettled him again.

The client project's storm had calmed, yet the office was far from peaceful.
Whispers spread: *"Sora's looking more and more like Riku's successor."*
Others muttered: *"He talks in frameworks, but when it comes to execution—it's still us carrying the load."*

Even Haru, once always beside him, now felt slightly distant.
They collaborated more than ever, but laughter between them was rare.

Sora's chest sometimes tightened:

"I see the roots. But not the people around me."

2. The Assignment

The new quarter brought a cross-department integration project—
to unify sales data across three regions and link it with logistics systems.

Riku tossed the task at him with no hesitation: *"You lead it."*
No encouragement, no discussion—just a command.

A weight dropped squarely on Sora's shoulders.
This was no longer analyst's work; it was coordination.

The kickoff meeting froze almost at once.
The East team's head snapped: *"Headquarters always assumes too much. We can't just copy-paste."*

The South rep sneered: *"Who guarantees your model? When it breaks, who takes the blame?"*

The air was as stiff as ice.
Haru took notes but stayed silent.

Afterwards, he sighed: *"You know what people say? That you look more and more like someone above—someone who doesn't see their struggles."*

Sora flinched.
He wanted to defend himself, but no words came.

3. Haru's Distance

Weeks passed. Haru still worked beside him, yet a faint detachment edged his tone.
When Sora pitched a "bigger vision," Haru merely answered, *"Mm,"* without the old habit of filling in details.

One late night, after they grabbed onigiri at the convenience store, Haru said:
"Your words now—always 'strategy,' 'trend.' They sound big. But who's hauling the boxes? Who's burning midnight oil fixing numbers? They think you've drifted far."

Sora stayed quiet, squeezing the rice ball till its shape collapsed.
He realized—
he had fallen back into his old flaw of "seeing mountains but not trees."
This time, it wore a different mask.

4. The Old Man Again

Friday night, he walked once more up the mountain road.
Cold wind whipped the stones slick, yet the hut's lantern still glowed.

The old man sat on the steps, tea steaming in his palms.
Sora sat too, blurting before the other could speak: *"I think I've lost the path again."*
The old man gazed into the night.
"Have you seen a forest in the wind?"

Sora nodded.

"A lone tree bends. But in a forest, trees shield each other."
The man's voice moved like wind through branches.
"Wisdom without action is an empty thought. Action without union is a lone trunk. True practice isn't how straight you stand, but whether your roots intertwine with others. Only a forest withstands the wind."

Sora's eyes widened.
He recalled the quarrels in team meetings, Haru's look of weariness.

All this time he had focused only on *his own roots*, forgetting the power of *union*.

He whispered: *"Speed doesn't come from one man running— it's when everyone walks steady together."*

The old man nodded. *"Achievement is not a personal 'higher rank,' but the force of a group joined as one."*

The lantern shook once in the breeze.
The old man added: *"Action is the step beneath your feet. Union is the direction of shoulders aligned."*

5. The Team in the Wind

Next day, Sora reconvened the cross-department group.
This time, he didn't begin with a grand vision.
He asked each leader to write their "potholes" on the whiteboard.

They appeared one by one:

- East: store reports delayed, logistics bottlenecks.
- South: definitions misaligned with HQ, often misunderstood.
- West: short on staff, execution lagging.

Sora offered no rebuttal. He simply noted them carefully.
Then he said: *"These are not your failures. They're roots we must repair—together."*
He proposed a shared board: whoever spotted a problem would mark it, and the right team would claim it.

"Not me alone watching—but all of us, together."

The room's air eased for the first time.
Someone said: *"Fine. I'll put East's delays on it first."*
Another nodded: *"Count us in."*

Haru, off to the side, let slip a small smile.

6. Conflict and Fracture

But harmony was brief.
By the third week, a client flagged a glaring error in data definitions.
The client now doubted the whole system.

Riku slammed his hand down: *"Who's responsible?!"*

Everyone lowered their eyes.
But glances slid inevitably toward Sora.

After the meeting, Haru confronted him:
"If you hadn't rushed it forward, this mistake wouldn't have happened."

Sora's face drained pale.
He wanted to protest, but the words died.
It was true: eager to prove "union," he hadn't given the team time to mend.

That night, walking alone in the cold, he finally understood:
**Action and union are not just about saying 'together.'
They demand a rhythm of steps.**

7. Repair

Days later, he sought Haru out.

"That mistake—it was mine. I was too hasty." He met Haru's eyes.
"I forgot: union doesn't mean others keep pace with me. It means I slow down, so we walk together."

Haru watched him for a few seconds, then smiled faintly: *"Good. As long as you know."*

After a pause, Haru extended his hand. *"Then let's start again."*

Sora grasped it.
That handshake felt heavier than any KPI.

8. The Old Man's Tea

Weekend again, he climbed the mountain.
The old man handed him a cup. On the tea's surface, shadows of tree upon tree overlapped.

"What do you see today?" the old man asked.

Sora studied the cup.
"Not a lone tree. Not just a forest. But many trees standing together, breaking the wind."

The old man nodded, a smile flickering in his eyes.
"Action and union—this is Rokudan."

The wind brushed past. The lantern swayed.
But it still burned steady.

Inside, Sora felt a new certainty:
Rank is not an individual's height, but the strength of many, joined as one.

Chapter Eight · Nanadan — Return and Restart

1. The Newcomer

After the New Year's bells faded, Tokyo's air carried a sharp winter freshness.
The streets were plastered with *hatsu-uri* (New Year sale) posters; people hurried by with lucky bags in their hands.

The office, too, welcomed several new faces.
One of them, a young man named **Takuya**, was assigned to the data team.

On his very first meeting, he sat nervously in the corner, clutching a stack of papers.
When his turn came, his voice was barely audible:

"Um... I recalculated the numbers... they should be correct."

Riku frowned.

"Just being correct isn't enough. You have to interpret."

The air froze.
Sora looked at Takuya and suddenly saw his younger self:
focused only on trees, blind to the forest; busy calculating, too afraid to look up.

2. A Shadow

That evening, Sora bumped into Takuya at a convenience store, buying rice balls.

The young man kept his head down, as if avoiding acquaintances.

Sora spoke: "Getting used to things?"

Takuya hesitated, then muttered, "Mm... It's just too much pressure. Feels like whatever I do, it's wrong."

Sora was silent for a moment, then handed him a hot canned coffee.
"You know, I've been there too. Back then, all I cared about was getting the numbers right. The more I calculated, the more exhausted I became—and still, no one was satisfied."

Takuya looked up, surprise flashing in his eyes.
In that instant, Sora understood:

The path he once walked, someone else was now repeating.

3. The Elder's Absence

On Friday night, he once again walked up the mountain path.
The wind was cold, the lantern at the cabin still glowed.
But this time, the elder was not sitting on the steps.

Only two empty cups sat on the tea table.
The lantern's shadow swayed lightly in the wind.

Sora felt a jolt in his chest.
He sat down as he had countless times before—yet for the first time realized:
The elder might not always be there, waiting.

The empty cups seemed to remind him:
Some lessons were already within him, needing no repetition.

4. Leading

The project entered a critical stage.
Takuya was tasked with preparing a regional data analysis.
But during the client meeting, someone challenged it:
"Your comparisons aren't rigorous. Metrics aren't unified."

Takuya's face flushed crimson; he froze.
Awkward silence filled the room.

Sora stepped forward, broke the problem apart, and rebuilt the logic.
The client remained cool, but finally nodded: "Next time, be careful."

Afterward, Takuya was on the verge of tears.
"I'm sorry. I held everyone back."

Sora shook his head.
"No—it's that we didn't give you time to grow roots."
Then he added quietly:
"Wisdom without action is empty thought; action without union is a lone tree."

As he said it, he realized:
These were no longer merely the elder's teachings.
They had become lessons he could pass on.

5. Haru's Reminder

One evening, Sora and Haru walked side by side near the subway entrance.
Haru suddenly said:
"You know, you look a lot like Zen now."

Sora blinked. "You've met him?"

Haru smiled faintly. "No. But I can see it—you've become, in others' eyes, the one sitting on the steps."

Sora said nothing.
His chest tightened with a bittersweet warmth.

6. Restart

At the end of the month, Takuya approached Sora:

"Could you help me check this report?"

Sora nodded.
But instead of correcting it himself, he asked Takuya to explain his thought process step by step.

"Slower, no rush," Sora said.

"Speed doesn't come from one person sprinting. It comes from the team walking steadily together."

Takuya repeated the line under his breath, as if engraving it into memory.

At that moment, Sora felt something unusual—
He was no longer just a traveler, but also a guide.

7. The Cabin Dream

That night, he dreamed of the cabin.
The lantern glowed as always; the elder sat on the steps, offering him a cup of tea.

"What do you see today?"

Sora answered:
"Not myself—but another, a shadow of who I once was."

The elder smiled.
"A shadow, one day, also becomes a lantern."

The wind blew, the lantern swayed gently.
When he awoke, he could still hear the trace of wind beside his pillow.

Epilogue

Spring was near.
On the streets, ginkgo trees sprouted new buds.

Sora gazed out the window and suddenly understood:
Ranks are not a staircase rising ever upward, but a cycle.

To reach the seventh stage is not "higher."
It is a "return"—to guide another along the road once walked.

This is the restart.

Chapter Nine · Hachidan — Emptiness

Space · Non-Attachment · Like the Wind

1. Broken Appointment

One sudden warm day before spring in Tokyo.
The wind thinned the clouds, the sky a washed-blue.
Sora arrived ten minutes early at the client's headquarters for the monthly review.
He tested the projector, flipped to the last slide, where he had carefully written his closing line—

> "When a leaf turns, the light of a tree changes; when a tree turns, the wind of a forest shifts."

> The door opened. Before anyone sat down, the secretary's phone rang:

> "Apologies, the executives have an emergency meeting. This session is canceled."

> The screen went black.
> Sora stood frozen, his hand still on the clicker, like a clock whose battery had run out.
> He expected to feel disappointment, even anger.
> Instead his chest felt hollow, with only a faint bewilderment—

> Everything prepared suddenly had no recipient.

> Leaving the room, he didn't send an update, didn't draft a follow-up.
> He simply walked down the stairs.
> One floor, two, until he reached the lobby, where sunlight flooded through the glass doors.
> He realized: this was a rare **gap of emptiness**.

He pulled out his phone, ready to pack the afternoon full—visits, reports, alignments.
Then he stopped. If every space was filled, where would emptiness live?

He switched the phone off, slipped it into his bag, and stepped into the sunlight.

2. Sea

He boarded a train heading south.
Buildings thinned, woods appeared, until suddenly the sea broke into view, a shard of celadon lifted by the wind.

The wind at Enoshima was sharper than in the city.
On the sand, a kite tugged its string into the sky, a curve stretched between hand and cloud.
Sora walked along the seawall, each heel strike against stone clear and decisive.
No destination, only the weight of steps given to the ground.

On the breakwater, he sat watching a tiny white boat on the horizon.
The wind folded and smoothed the waves, as though ironing and crumpling the same cloth again and again.

Busy and idle, gain and loss, presence and absence—all like folds of that cloth.
He realized many of his old attachments were nothing more than ripples in the sea breeze.

The phone buzzed in his pocket.
He looked—it was the team chat, pushing for the updated milestone chart.
He slid the phone back. *Later is fine.*
For the first time, he allowed a message to stay unread, as though permitting a leaf not to turn just yet.

3. Empty Room

That evening in Kamakura, he found a small inn halfway up the hill.
A polished wooden floor, paper-shaded lamp, low bed, and a window opening to a reddened sky.

He set down his bag.
The room felt like a blank page, so quiet he could hear the whisper of his sleeve brushing the floor.
Unease stirred.
He was used to rooms crammed with books, laptops, to-do lists.
Here, the emptiness itself pressed against him.

He tried to write. Pen against paper, yet no ink flowed.
He stopped. *Perhaps today, nothing needs to be written.*

He recapped the pen, pushed open the window.
The sea glimmered silver in moonlight, the breeze salty and damp.
He leaned against the frame, doing nothing but watching.

Emptiness is not absence—it is space left unfilled.

4. Dream

That night he dreamt of the mountain hut.
The lantern swayed. The old man sat as always, handing him a cup of tea.
The tea reflected stars, the eaves like a brushstroke never lifted.

Neither spoke.
They sat together as wind slipped beneath the eaves.
Presence, without the need for words.

He woke at dawn.

The breeze light, the clouds thin, the sea flat as glass.

5. Bowl

Breakfast came on a tray: rice, miso soup, grilled fish, small vegetables.
As he lifted the bowl, he noticed a fine chip along its rim—
not new, not obvious, but like time's fingerprint on porcelain.

He ran his thumb across it and felt an odd tenderness.
Incompletion gave the bowl humanity.
Once he had polished everything toward perfection.
Now, he accepted this flaw as one accepts the hollow in one's own heart.

He thought of work—the data never fully aligned, the processes never entirely punctual, the colleagues who sometimes erred.
Perhaps the world needn't be smoothed to perfection.
A little roughness reminds the hand it is still touching reality.

6. Lines

On the train back, he opened and closed his bag, then left the phone shut another hour.
Nearby, an elderly couple murmured, children laughed.
Power lines streamed backward outside, like rulers etching invisible lines across sky and earth.

He stared at his hands.
A childhood scar on one, calluses from months of typing and hauling cases on the other.
Each mark, proof of being.

He thought: maybe his team too needed blank space.
Not every box filled, not every task closed the same day.

Space is where things can grow.

7. Empty Meeting

Monday morning, he booked a "small meeting." Only himself entered the room.
He projected the screen, then turned it off again, letting the wall return to white.

"Today's agenda: no agenda."
He wrote the words on the board and laughed.

Ten minutes passed. Nothing happened.
At twenty, he poured water.
At thirty, he stared at the blank wall—
it blurred into a lake, still enough to reflect his own shadow.

Once, he did to secure certainty.
Today, he didn't do, to see.
He wiped the board clean. Left nothing.
Walking out, his body felt lighter.

8. Takuya's Report

That afternoon, Takuya brought a report.
"I cut most of the tables, just three pages," he admitted nervously.

Sora flipped through:
Page 1: the problem.
Page 2: the causes.
Page 3: the next steps.

No clutter of numbers, no empty slogans.

"Good." Sora smiled. "Cut what's unnecessary, let the essential speak."

Takuya exhaled, then whispered: "The empty parts are the ones people remember."

Emptiness had taken the shape of memory.

9. Haru's Joke

That evening Haru dropped two hot coffees on Sora's desk. "You've been spacing out today."

"Really?" Sora grinned.
"Yeah—but not lazy. More like..." Haru searched for words, "like you cleared the table, leaving room for us to sit."

Sora stared. "That's a compliment?"
"Reminder," Haru said, mock-stern. "Don't fill the empty seat again."

They both laughed.
And Sora thought: perhaps emptiness isn't only for oneself, but also for others.

10. Uncertainty

A week later, the group decided to expand their pilot to more regions.
The team cheered, but Sora didn't pop champagne.
On the task board, he drew a new column, labeled it: **Uncertainty**.

"What's that for?" someone asked.
"For what's not on the list," he said.

"The wind will rise, leaves will fall, algorithms will change, logistics will delay—something always arrives outside our plans.
This is its place. Once we see it, we needn't fear it."

Fear, once given a visible box, ceases to be only fear.

11. Mountain Path

Friday night he returned to the northern exit.
The wind was mild, the lamps cast warm light.
Gravel crunched steady beneath his steps, like a metronome.

The hut still stood. Lantern steady.
The old man nodded as Sora approached.
He handed tea. Neither spoke.

They sat as time thinned to a slow stream under the eaves.

At last, the old man murmured: "The wind is light."
Sora nodded: "The sea is light too."

The old man smiled: "Sometimes, not speaking is also speaking."
Sora tucked the words into his chest, lowering his lamp.

He saw in his mind:
Trees standing in wind. Roots asleep in earth. Mountains watching afar. Sea breathing near.
None needed his control. Each had its rhythm.

When the tea cooled, the old man took the cup back, set it on the step.
"Go," he said. No advice, no farewell. Just: **"Go."**

Sora bowed, descended.
He knew now—presence could be as if absence.
He no longer needed to return for words.
The lamp was already within him.

12. White Space

Back in the city, Sora opened his laptop to draft next quarter's plan.
He typed the title, pressed enter—one blank line, two, three…
A quiet whiteness spread across the screen.

He wrote the first line:
"Uncertainty is part of planning."

Then the second:
"White space is part of action."

The cursor blinked at the edge like breathing.

Emptiness is not retreat, but letting "having" breathe.
Emptiness is not void, but letting the Way flow.

He saved, stretched, and looked outside.
The clouds had parted, a square of blue revealed.
The air shone, like glass freshly cleaned.

13. Return

That weekend, he didn't visit the hut or the sea.
He went to the small park near home, sat on a sunlit bench.
Children chased, old men played chess, a dog dozed in shade.

Life was made of such moments never written in reports.
He realized: emptiness was not escape, but return to being.

His phone buzzed.
He glanced, smiled, replied:
"See you next week. We'll walk slowly."
Pocketing it, he leaned back, closed his eyes.
Wind brushed his brow like a gentle hand.

Epilogue · Emptiness

That night he dreamt a short dream.
No hut, no lantern, no tea.
Only a mountain path, empty of people.
Wind moved, shadows of trees crossed and shifted.
The scent of sea lingered far away.

He woke. The same square of blue sky outside.
One word came: **Emptiness**.

Not nothingness. Not avoidance. But **non-attachment**

- Not clinging to every meeting.
- Not demanding every report be perfect.
- Not insisting every answer appear at once.

Withdrawing the hand from control, the eye from anxiety,
letting trees, mountains, roots, winds, seas, and people all hold their place.

And softly, in his heart, he said:

"I am here. That is enough."

Epilogue · Ninth Dan (Kyūdan) — No Dan

Stillness · Softness · Steadiness

1. Morning in the Park

Sunday morning, the wind still carried a trace of the night's chill.
Sora sat on a park bench, a cup of warm water at his side.

Elderly people passed by during their morning exercises; some nodded, some greeted him.
He simply smiled in return, eyes clear, unhurried.

Children chased each other on the grass, kites rising and dipping in the wind.
One child fell, cried briefly, then quickly got up and continued to run.
Sora watched quietly, the corners of his mouth curving slightly.
No words were spoken, but in his heart he nodded: **falling, too, is part of walking.**

2. Silence in the Office

Monday's meeting was as tense as ever.
Numbers fluctuated on the screen, and Riku's brow furrowed deeply.

One voice rose: "This model isn't stable, the risk is too high."
Another countered: "If we don't try, we'll never have results."

73

The air froze, and everyone's eyes turned to Sora.

He didn't speak right away.
Instead, he opened his notebook and gently slid a page to the center of the table:
a sketch of a tree, its roots spread wide, its branches open.
Beside it, a few simple lines:

"Do not rush to grow tall.
Let the roots be steady.
The wind will pass."

No long arguments, no debates.
The meeting room fell silent for a few seconds, voices slowly subsiding.
Even Riku only gave a brief "hmm," which was enough to count as approval.

3. The Yellow Light of a Convenience Store

Late at night after overtime, he stepped into the convenience store downstairs.
The light above the register was dim, the cashier stifling a yawn.

Sora bought a cup of hot milk.
At checkout, the cashier's hand slipped, and coins scattered across the floor.

He crouched down, picking up each coin one by one, and placed them back in the tray.
No words of "it's fine," just a quiet action completed.

The cashier blinked, then smiled.
That smile was like a small lamp, lighting up the night for a moment.

4. The Wind on the Mountain Path

On Friday night, he once again walked the mountain path at the north exit.
The lantern still glowed, but the space before the wooden house was empty.

He did not search.
He simply stood in the wind, lifting his eyes toward the mountain.

The wind passed, tossing his hair, stirring the shadows of the branches.
His gaze was soft, yet without a trace of panic.
His heart was like a steady stone, letting the wind swirl around it.

He whispered to himself:

"The Dans are complete, but the road is not."

Then he turned to descend the mountain.
His steps were neither fast nor slow, light upon the ground, yet each one firm.

5. The Person of No Dan

From then on, Sora was no longer conspicuous among people.
He no longer rushed to speak first, nor strained to prove himself.

He listened quietly, spoke gently, sometimes responding only with a glance.
Colleagues found themselves surprised: his eyes were soft, yet gave a sense of steadiness.

Like a tree—
no matter how strong the wind, no matter how restless the branches,

the trunk remained calm and unmoved.

"Dan, is not Dan.
Having, is not having.
Walking, is already arriving home."

Afterword

At first, my intention was simple.
During a period of deep collaboration with Japanese companies, I often observed the challenges faced by new colleagues.
I only wanted to write something small, to communicate better, to share some experiences and reflections with them.
I never planned to make it into a book.

But once words are written down, they grow like seeds.
I realized these fragments were not just for one situation —
they could be read more widely,
and mirrored against the inner journey of many others.

So this is not a book of "answers" written for others,
but a record of my own path of practice.

Now that it is in your hands,
it is no longer only my story.
It may reflect parts of your own journey.

If, between the lines of these pages,
you catch a glimpse of your own heart,
then *Nine Dans of Awakening* has fulfilled its most important mission.

— ButterflyMan

www.ingramcontent.com/pod-product-compliance
Lightning Source LLC
LaVergne TN
LVHW052341080426
835508LV00045B/3282